OUR SUMMER IN ALASKA, 1917

Michael, Huberta, Grandfather and Grandmother Rourke and Dog Gyp in front of Glacier Station, Alaska along the White Pass and Yukon Railroad.

OUR SUMMER IN ALASKA, 1917

by Huberta Swensen

LYNN CANAL PUBLISHING
Skagway, Alaska

ISBN: 0-945284-02-0

Lynn Canal Publishing
P.O. Box 1898, 264 Broadway
Skagway, Alaska 99840-0498

Printed in U.S.A.

TABLE OF CONTENTS

Author Huberta Swensen disembarks from the cruise ship *Daphne* on her return visit to Skagway, Alaska in 1988. *Costa Cruises*

FOREWORD

A number of people helped Huberta Swensen retrace her steps in the process of writing this book. White Pass and Yukon Railroad historian Carl Mulvihill was invaluable in clearing up some facts about the railway and its history. Valerie Lawson, former director of the City of Skagway's Trail of '98 Museum, also assisted the author during her return visit to Skagway in 1988. Many of the photos in this book, along with others in her collection, were donated to the museum.

Huberta arrived in Skagway on board the cruise ship *Daphne*, and many of the passengers and crew on board the ship listened to her story of the trip up the Inside Passage in 1917. They encouraged her to finish the book. Huberta was in Skagway only a few hours, just long enough to visit the museum and read the manuscript to us in the back room of our book store. It was a busy day, and many visitors stopped to listen. We knew right away that this was a special story.

Jeff and Diane Brady
Lynn Canal Publishing
March, 1991
Skagway, Alaska

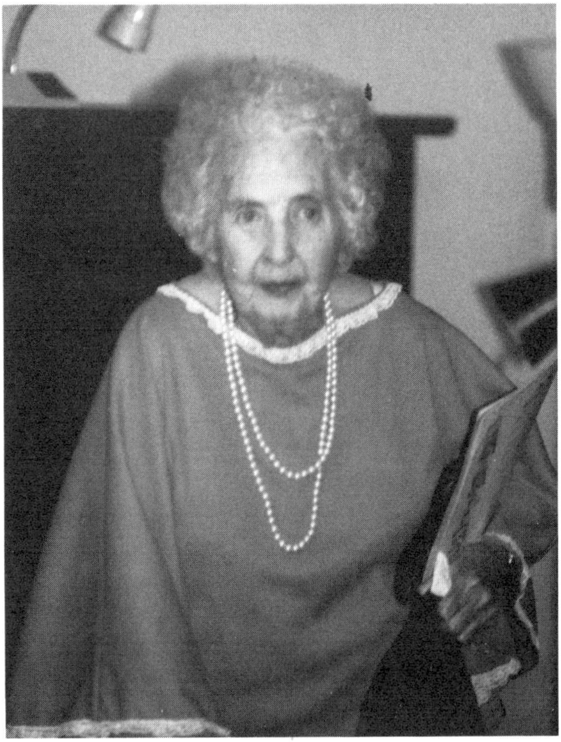

Author Huberta Swensen

INTRODUCTION

Not many of today's children have the privilege of being prepared for a visit to Alaska. The last frontier is a much richer and beautiful land if you study it before you go there.

As young children, my brother, Michael Rourke, and I spent two summers with our grandparents, James and Emma Rourke, near Skagway, Alaska. The memory of the first summer in 1913 is not as vivid as the second in 1917, perhaps because our mother, Rosa Pearl Rourke, prepared us better beforehand. She taught us all about the history, geography and geology of the Inside Passage to Skagway. Those first lessons made the experience more meaningful and the memories more lasting.

Sailing on steamships was a new adventure for two children who had never seen a body of water larger than the swimming natorium at the hot springs resort near our home in Idaho. At the end of the Inside Passage, the White Pass and Yukon Railroad cut through mountains of solid rock above the old Trail of '98. This was to be our territory, just nineteen years after the great Klondike Gold Rush.

Mother recorded the summer with her camera, developing the black and white, postcard-sized pictures beside the trail in the spirit of the great photographers of the Klondike stampede. It is my sincere hope that the stories built from those pictures will convey all the beauty and nostalgic memories of that time — when the boats plying the Inside Passage were powered by steam and when the great iron horses belched smoke on the high trestles of the White Pass, making the rails sing on the single-gauge tracks.

Mother taught us how to explore and learn. This story is seen through the eyes of her camera and her two lively children.

Huberta Swensen
March, 1991
Seattle, Washington

Huberta's father, Charles Nanney, in brakeman's uniform (above), and working on the Oregon Short Line of the Union Pacific in Southeastern Idaho. He was later promoted to conductor.

1

A Golden Transportation Era

We were born into the golden era of railroads and steamships. The magic of the rails, the big iron horses and plush coaches with red seats were all part of growing up. We were used to superb dining car service, the Pullman sleeping car accommodations, and, on longer trips, the relaxing observation cars.

After these many years, I still see in my dreams the early-century trains and hear the whistles and bells. Dad is teaching us the meanings of the whistle signals — the combinations of the longs and shorts — whose accuracy was never to be mistaken by the engineer in the cabin, the signalman at the crossing, the fireman feeding the firebox, the brakeman turning the brake wheels atop the cars, and the conductor at his post in the caboose.

My father, Charles Nanney, was a railroad man, and home was a small-town oasis in the middle of Idaho. It was a sparsely inhabited and unirrigated country when we were growing up. The railroad was a big part of our lives.

In the second decade of the century, we were to learn about another railroad in a different kind of country. Our Grandfather served on a railroad in Alaska, and in 1917 our vacation home was to be a large red station house in the wilderness.

Our grandparents were sourdoughs, a name for residents who have spent many years pioneering Alaska. They knew and understood the country well and had sent books and maps for us to read and study during the winter of 1916-1917. As soon as school closed in June, we boarded the train in Idaho, "All Aboard" for our big adventure.

Our train was late arriving in Seattle, Washington. After the shock of discovering we had missed our connection from train to boat, Mother waved her magic wand and changed that happening to one of pleasure and education. She always had a happy way of surmounting disappointment.

We were frightened and lonely small-town people destined to spend six days in what seemed an enormously big city with noisy, clanging streetcars and cable trolleys. Our hotel was not far from the Yesler Way cable line and historic Pioneer Square.

The totem pole standing so erect there seemed sinister to country children, and Mother bought small ones for us. We tried to decipher the legendary meanings of the carved characters.

We learned that Northwest Indian lore taught that the raven was the father of all. He seemed to be looking down on his Indian children of mother earth as they crafted and sold their wares in the triangle encompassing the tall, uniquely carved totem pole.

We went for a streetcar ride to Green Lake and became motion sick, so we disembarked and walked until we felt settled enough to board again. Mother remarked that it was strange that we became ill on a streetcar when we had never had any trouble on trains — even when it had been necessary to occupy an upper berth in the Pullman sleeping car. Mother would settle the argument between Brother and I over who slept on the top. She would have us draw straws, and the short straw took the upper.

Mother always requested the Pullman car attendant to make our berths down feet-first, which was opposite of the regular practice at that time. All of us did better in the "going" position and sleeping in the same way with our feet out in front of us, pointing toward the front of the train.

After six days of exploring the beautiful city of Seattle on Puget Sound, a steamship reservation was available, and we

Union Pacific trains arrived at the Oregon and Washington Station (now called Union Station) on King Street, shown here in 1911.

Seattle Museum of History and Industry

walked up the gangplank and were off to months of thrilling sights that only Alaska had to offer. I doubt if there are any more beautiful trips in the world than the boat trip between Seattle and Skagway on the Inside Passage.

While on my recent trip in 1988, a constantly changing panoramic view kept me in a daze of rapture and fascination while sitting comfortably at one of the view windows in the lounge or walking on the deck.

My cabin bed was made down in the head-first position. I left it that way and no motion sickness occurred — perhaps because most of the time on the cruise ship, I was not conscious of movement.

Mother took this picture of a glacier on the trip up the Inside Passage.

Ketchikan was a busy gateway city for ships coming north to Alaska. This view of the west part of the city is taken from a postcard purchased on the 1917 journey.

2

Cruising the Inside Passage

Steaming up Alaska's Inside Passage imprinted me with indelible ink, never-to-be-forgotten exotic memories. Viewing fjord-indented coasts augmented with glistening glaciers, abrupt mountains and dense forests provided a sweet nectar of relaxation as we reclined comfortably or walked the decks. Seventy-one years later, I perceived and experienced all that beauty in the same manner.

Early travelers had a choice of the Canadian Pacific or the Alaska Steamship lines. Air flights and the Alcan Highway were, of course, unknown in 1917. Going via boat was the only transportation. Accommodations and food on both lines were excellent and the service gracious, personal and pleasant.

The Alaska Steamship boats would leave Seattle, making the ports of Ketchikan and Juneau en route north. Both communities were thriving in 1917.

Ketchikan was situated on very mountainous terrain. It must have been difficult to find land suitable for air travel landings and takeoffs in this country where the mountains met the sea. Ketchikan's airport today is on an island across from that little city. Passengers commute between the mainland and the air strip — a very short distance via a small ferry.

There were other stops. Sometimes boats docked at the old Russian capital of Sitka. The United States purchased Alaska from Russia in 1867, but the Russian culture was still visible. Passengers would visit the beautiful little Russian church to view the religious icons and works of art enshrined there. The church suffered a fire since we first visited Alaska, but the priceless works of art were saved and the church was reconstructed.

Awe-inspiring sights visible from ship deck were educational and thrilling to view. Sea gulls followed the ship to feast on the scraps from the kitchen, maneuvering gracefully in flight to reach the choice morsels. Few sea gulls follow the ships today. In this modern scientific age, kitchen and table residue are no doubt disposed of according to environmental protection regulations.

Sometimes we would see whales cavorting playfully, surfacing to spout their fountains of spray. They were beautiful. I loved and admired them then and still read everything I find on the history of these great creatures, whose ancestry goes back hundreds of millions of years.

Icebergs which had broken away from glaciers floated precariously near the ship at times. When the sun was shining on them, they glistened with a bluish hue, and their beauty was breathtaking, camouflaging the potential of treachery that lay beneath the surface.

In 1917, we waited at Wrangell Narrows for the tide to be right before proceeding slowly. Getting through the channel took time, as there was a big rock in the middle of the north passageway which had to be bypassed. This rock has since been removed, but our cruise ship in 1988 still moved cautiously through the passage.

The skippers of the Alaskan passages know their waters well. There were some shipwrecks in the early part of this century, but we don't hear of them in this age of modern, safe travel.

The two ships which took us to Alaska, the *State of California* in 1913 and the *Princess Sophia* in 1917, afterward went down.

The *State of California*, owned by Pacific Coast Steamship Company and under the command of Captain Thomas H. Cann, sank on August 17, 1913 after striking an uncharted reef in Gambier Bay between Juneau and Admiralty Island. Thirty-five persons drowned, but one hundred eleven were saved. The ship sank only four minutes away from the dock at Gambier Bay.

The *Princess Sophia*, stuck on Vanderbilt Reef, before she perished in this terrible storm. *Winter & Pond Collection • Alaska State Library*

How grateful we are in this day and age to walk up the gangplank knowing we will be secure and safe. Marine science then could not always measure the accuracy of a shifting ocean floor, and there were yet-to-be-discovered and uncharted reefs and rocks which were hazardous to safe travel along the Inside Passage.

The crystal chandelier at the foot of the beautiful staircase to the dining room of the *Princess Sophia* was gorgeous. Two growing, always hungry children loved the delicacies of afternoon tea and would prevail upon Mother to let us stay up for midnight buffet so we could eat again.

We were saddened to learn of the *Sophia*'s sinking on October 25, 1918 and the tremendous loss of life. That beautiful little ship had left Skagway on October 22 with two hundred sixty-nine passengers and a crew of seventy-four. She struck Vanderbilt Reef in a freak snow storm near Juneau. Initially all aboard were presumed safe, and it was hoped that the ship could float off the reef. The ship called off rescue efforts until it was too late. The storm worsened, and the ship went down. No one survived.

Years after the tragedy, I met a fishing boat captain who had heard the final S.O.S. distress signals from the *Sophia*. They went as soon as possible but did not arrive in time. His and the crew's sordid task was to pick up the frozen bodies, which were doubled over with cramps, and put them on deck to take into port. He cried when he told me about it, and I cried too.

We had such a happy trip on the *Sophia*, and we remembered very well the charm of the personnel and their kindness to two active children.

One morning, while in the dining room for breakfast, Brother showed us how much he had learned to read. Mother would help him make his choices from his very own table menu — with her approval of course.

The waiter said, "Has our young man made his selection yet?" He had. "I'll have fruits in season, please," was the reply. The waiter smilingly replied, "I'll see what I can do. There are not too many fruits in season at one time." The result was a big bowl of oranges, apples and bananas set

A postcard view of totem poles at a Southeast Alaska Indian village.

before that wide-eyed little boy. He never forgot the fun of it.

We were seasick only once during the entire trip. While going through Queen Charlotte Sound, the waves had been round and big, unusual for that time of year. No passengers had been in the dining room for lunch that day, and the ship's nurse kept busy going from one passenger to another who needed her help.

As I look at the pictures taken then and remember the boats we traveled on in the second decade of the century, I draw the comparison of the difference in size and tonnage of the boats. Ships were smaller then, carrying less than five hundred passengers, whereas most of today's ships are more like ocean liners with upwards of one thousand passengers on board.

The first years of our century had been difficult for pioneering our great country in the West. Then the gold rush of 1898 opened up the "New Frontier" to the north. Alaska remained a territory until it became the forty-ninth state on January 3, 1959. Transportation had to undergo experimentation in virgin country and in sailing unfamiliar waters.

When cruising the Inside Passage in 1913 and 1917, we would sometimes see an Indian cemetery on an island or on the mainland, where the dead were buried in the tops of the trees. To discourage predators, the limbs had been cut.

One time little brother said, "Mama, what are those big pincushions doing over there?"

In southeastern Alaska, various heights of totem poles would identify an occasional clearing as an Indian fishing village. Some totem poles of the North American Indians of the Pacific Coast are used as grave markers. Others were scattered through Native villages. Quite often they were attached to houses and signified legendary and real events in the lives of the owners.

Brother, always the curious and observing one, never hesitated to ask questions, and Mother would patiently answer as best she could.

That time she told him that there were dead bodies buried in the tops of the trees, and the lower limbs had been cut away so animals could not get up to the bodies. She said, "There would never be need for a pincushion that large."

Parade guards and guests at Fort Seward in Port Chilkoot near Haines during World War One.

Years later when we were reminiscing about our 1917 Alaska adventures, Brother and I discussed the incident and how Mother was always so patient in going into details of a subject. We both agreed that children's optical illusions are sometimes very exaggerated in size and stature, and association with an object you are already familiar with is very characteristic.

She had further explained, "You remember the picnics we went on in Idaho, don't you? Where sometimes we would find an old Indian cemetery — the dead of the Bannock tribe of the Blackfoot Indians in Idaho near our home town were buried in the ground with their possessions, so they would have them in the 'Happy Hunting Ground' of their hereafter. Sometimes we found arrow flints and other artifacts. So, as those Indians buried their dead in the ground, the Indians on the shores we see have buried their dead high in the tops of the trees."

That satisfied him.

Death had been explained to us in our early years. Dad was the second eldest in a family of ten brothers and sisters, and we had many aunts, uncles and cousins. The grandparents' farm was the gathering place for occasions of joy and also of sorrow. Many times the bodies were laid out in the parlor of the family farm house before burial. So death was no stranger to us in pioneer days.

Onward we went toward Skagway, noting and cataloging in our memories the many sights and sounds, all so different from our Idaho home.

After passing Fort Seward, a large army base and fort in the World War One year of 1917, we were almost to our next port, Skagway. Mother did the packing as we neared our destination.

Above, a postcard view of Skagway, Alaska in 1917. The X marks Inspiration Point on the WP&YR. Right, Brother Michael Rourke and Dog Gyp at Clifton Station on the railroad.

3

Skagway, Alaska and Clifton Station

Our arrival in Skagway was a grand reunion of hugs and kisses with everyone talking at once, not caring much about what was said. Being together was all that mattered. More serious communication would come later.

The first excitement over, Grandmother said, "I have shopping and ordering of supplies to do in town, so we won't take the train to Clifton until day after tomorrow. I've made reservations at the Golden North for our rooms and meals while we are here. We will visit with George and Clara Dedman."

The Dedmans helped establish the original Golden North Hotel during the gold rush and later expanded it into a new building, which they moved in 1908 to its present location in the center of town.

"Next time we come in, we will stay at the Pullen House," Grandmother added. "Mother Pullen can hardly wait to see how you've grown in four years. We'll go see her today. Now she has a ranch in Dyea with cows and a garden. There are fresh vegetables and milk for the tables."

"I'm glad," Brother said. "I don't like condensed milk on my oatmeal."

Mrs. Harriet Pullen, lovingly called the "Mother of the North," joined the gold rush in 1897. She died at the age of almost eighty-seven in 1947. The description of her in recent writings brought her back to my memory just as I had remembered her — always friendly, vibrant and enthusiastic.

Grandmother and Grandfather had many good friends in Skagway, to whom we were introduced. Gertrude Mulvihill, daughter of Nellie and William John "Mul" Mulvihill, chief dispatcher of the White Pass and Yukon Railroad, became my playmate during the summer of 1917. Her daughter, Barbara Fairbanks, told me that she passed away in 1967. Gertrude's nephew, Carl Mulvihill, a historian of the WP&YR, resides in Skagway, as do other family members. Her granddaughter, Valerie Feero Lawson, was curator in the city museum the day of my recent visit in 1988. She greeted me hospitably and drove me around that beautiful little town. The old Mulvihill home still stands sturdy and strong and is well-kept by Jeff and Diane Brady, publishers of this book.

Back to 1917. After visiting friends and seeing Grandmother's ordering completed, we were off to Clifton Station to greet Grandfather. He had been unable to leave his work as section foreman. Dear Dog Gyp had grieved for days after we had left in 1913, and his happiness at seeing us again was exciting.

Grandfather's greeting was warm and affectionate, and we wouldn't give him a minute's peace until he took us to see the playhouse he had created for us. He had reinforced an old bear cave in the side of the mountain below the station house. It was safe, and he had furnished it with doll beds, cupboards and chairs that he had made from boxes and painted white.

Once we were down the steep, precarious path to its entrance, we loved it. Everything that was chewable for the squirrels' nests had to be brought up to the station house every evening. We enjoyed our red squirrel neighbors, but they had no respect for others' property, and stealing was part of their game.

We were taught to identify bear tracks and did not linger long, nor complete a trip, if we saw any. However, we had been instructed not to fear them, but to stand still, looking directly at them. We never had to put those directions to use. Mother bears with their cubs often, when going

Huberta Swensen, left, with friend Gertrude Mulvihill, playing with dolls in Skagway.

through the area, would pass close by, and we would remain quiet where we were. Even though I'm sure Mother Bear sensed our nearness, she would go on her way with the cubs trailing close behind. She knew we would not harm them and was more intent on getting to the berries, which were everywhere — high and low bush cranberries, wild raspberries and blueberries — and the river was not far below.

Grandmother told us of her experience with a lone bear while she was picking berries. She was alone, with the rifle that Grandfather had insisted she carry lying on the ground beside her.

Who is calling the bluff? This popular postcard was our favorite from the journey of 1917.

She sensed a presence behind her, and turning her head slowly, looked into the face of a full-grown bear. Making no move toward the rifle, she stared into his eyes. He returned the gaze. They remained in that position for about three or four minutes, but she said it seemed much longer. During the long gaze she kept thinking, "I don't want to use this rifle — I don't want to hurt or kill any living creature. You are a magnificent fellow. Please leave."

And he did. Of course she knew that if she had made a move toward picking up the rifle, he would have attacked.

Grandmother had been born in a covered wagon with a wagon train working its way to the New West. Her parents had left devastation and poverty in Virginia in the aftermath of the Civil War.

Her father had stowed away on a boat from Germany to escape the compulsory military training in practice there and to find a new life in the New World for his family, which had suffered greatly from the famine of that period. He was discovered and put to work for his passage. When he left the ship, he went looking for work and found it in Virginia. Being a farm boy, well-educated and strong, he had no difficulty fitting into the life of a run-down estate to take the place of the sons who had been killed in the war. He became part of the family and fell in love with the daughter. They were married.

The West had opened for homesteading lands, so the family sold enough of their belongings to take a wagon train west. Grandmother was born en route near the Little Platte River in Nebraska. Her father took out extensive homestead lands in Wyoming for cattle raising and range.

Grandmother and her brother, Johnnie, grew up there together, riding the range. Grandmother imitated all the riding tricks that her brother had been practicing — until her strict German father discovered her riding while standing on two horses. One foot was on each horse, her long braids of hair flying in the wind, and nothing to hang on to but the single reins. A horse's hoof stumbling into a rabbit or gopher hole would have spelled disaster. A family conference was held, and Grandmother was sent away to girl's boarding school and later to take her nurse's training in Colorado. Johnnie afterward became a famous trick rider and traveled with Buffalo Bill's Wild West Show and the circuses for many years.

So Grandmother's experiences during her early years in the New West and her schooling and training all had equipped her for being a high-spirited, capable and loving wife, mother and grandmother with the ability to adjust to life in Alaska, the last frontier.

Grandfather too was strong in spirit and capability. He had a very brave start, having been born in a wild storm on the North Sea off Ireland. His mother was out to sea with her husband, an Irish sea captain. Grandfather's naturalization papers of Troy, New York read, "James Rourke, a native of Ireland in the Kingdom of Britain," and are dated October, 1876.

Grandfather followed the building of the railroads west, and he and Grandmother were married in Laramie, Wyoming on November 28, 1881. Our mother, Rosa Pearl Rourke, was their first-born on December 14, 1882 in Laramie City.

Rosa Pearl was a beautiful, high-spirited child who loved to dance. In 1898 the family was in Pueblo, Colorado and Rosa was in the school program at the end of the spring term.

Yet Mother very much resented having to move so often, as her "My Diary" of 1900 indicates:

> **Soda Springs, Idaho (Jan. 1st).** "This is New Years night and I have been very lonesome all day. We have been here just a week today and I have made no new acquaintances. There is a big masquerade party here tonight but I cannot go as I am not acquainted. This is the dullest New Years that I ever experienced and I sincerely hope that next year we will be where we are acquainted with a few people at least."

Five more children were born, all at different localities in the New West. Eugene Francis was born at Little Creek in Lincoln County, Washington on July 17, 1884. Lincoln Jay was born at the same place on October 23, 1885. James Harrison was born at Silver Bow in the Montana Territory on October 30, 1888.

Susan Elizabeth was born in Huerfano, Colorado on May 28, 1891. "Susie, the loved one," as Grandfather wrote in his family records, was not with them very long. She died in Soda Springs in 1901 from what was then called inflammation of the stomach. Medical science later discovered the appendix. but it was too late to save her life and many others who had been taken earlier.

"Marie," a beautiful antique doll, had been given to her. Many years later it was given to me. "Marie" has been my companion since childhood, and today she sits regally on her bird's-eye, maple rocking chair that my grandparents gave to me.

The sixth child, Annie Eliza, was born at Cuchara, Colorado on December 27, 1892.

Is it any wonder that Mother resented moving so often?

Grandmother Emma Rourke

Grandfather James Rourke

Gyp, the station dog, runs on the platform at Clifton. Mother took this picture on Sept. 1, 1917.

However, it had given her a spirit of restlessness. She was always searching out the adventures to be reaped from everyday happenings and travel. How she loved the summers with the grandparents in Alaska is well-demonstrated in her photography. She did all her own developing and finishing, and woe be to anyone who opened the door to the darkroom while she was processing. One streak of light would have ruined the whole strip as she ran it back and forth through the solution.

God love her memory. She was taken two years after our summer at Clifton during the tragic influenza epidemic of 1919.

Extrasensory perception qualities have always been very prevalent in our family. Mother had nursed us through the flu, then was stricken herself. Antibiotics were unknown and home remedies were not effective enough. Our Idaho town was struggling through with schools closed, many deaths, every family down and no nurse available. I was trying to give Mother a drink of water and she called out, "Mother, I need you — I need you." Grandmother received those ESP waves. She and Grandfather packed, and as soon as he could get relieved of his duties while away, they took a dog sled to Skagway, boat from Skagway to Seattle, and the flyer train from Seattle to Pocatello, Idaho. They were ten days in getting there, but one day, while they were walking on the decks of the boat, Grandmother said to Grandfather, "Pearl is gone." He said, "Yes, I knew five minutes ago." It was six minutes past noon. Mother had died at 12:01p.m. Strange but true.

Mother, Rosa Pearl Rourke, stands by a ruined building in the ghost town of White Pass City on the Trail of '98 between Clifton and the summit of the White Pass.

Now back to 1917 adventures. To greet us at Clifton beside Grandfather and Dog Gyp were some of the section crew and soldiers from Fort Seward near Haines. They were sent over each month to board and room at the station house while they guarded and patrolled the railroad tracks and bridges during the World War One years.

Grandmother and Mother were soon in their aprons with their hands in biscuit dough, and we were taken for a ride on the pushcar and a walk along the railroad tracks. The wonderful aromas came wafting toward us, and soon the dinner bell was ringing. After washing our hands we were all at the big, long table ready to eat.

The station house was not beautiful. It was large with rooms of high ceilings, barren floors scrubbed spotlessly clean, very few windows, but cheerful in Grandmother's ruffle curtains. A woman's touch was evident everywhere. With all the love and friendship, it was truly home for those who lived there year-round and those like us who were there for a short time.

Glacier Station had been the same for us in 1913, and Grandmother's many flower boxes all along the platform were a beautiful sight. Her pansy blossoms were as large as saucers. How could they be otherwise in the land where it was light all night and the soil a rich, black loam of decay from centuries past.

Brother and I were assigned helping-out duties, and one of them was to help with dishes and cleaning up the kitchen.

Our lessons in geology, geography and history would start the next day. We were in the midst of all that we had read and studied about during the winter before our departure to the land of the midnight sun. There would be only three months for everything planned, and so much to see.

A pushcar picnic along the WP&YR in 1917. From left, a railroad worker, Brother, Dog Gyp, Grandmother, Huberta, one of the soldiers who guarded the railroad, and Mother.

4

Life on the WP&YR

We had been brought up in railroading, so the White Pass and Yukon Railroad was of great interest to us. We had learned that this beautiful, scenic railway had been constructed in 1898-1900 with back-breaking labor, as there was no modern-day equipment then to get through mountains of solid rock to lay the single-gauge track. Blasting and dynamite and the use of pick and shovel had to accomplish that great feat.

It was 110.7 miles from terminal to terminal, Skagway, Alaska to Whitehorse, Yukon Territory, of which 20.4 miles are in Alaska, 32.2 miles in British Columbia, and 58.1 miles in the Yukon. Its summit at 2,865 feet is reached from sea level at Skagway in those first 20.4 miles. Golden spike ceremonies in Carcross, Yukon (Mile 67) on July 20, 1900 crowned its successful completion.

It was necessary for the section foreman and his men to spend long, tedious hours inspecting and clearing the narrow-gauge tracks of dirt and rock debris. Clifton, at Mile 8.6, was the first destination station out of Skagway. Glacier Station was the next stop at Mile 14.1.

Traveling on pushcars and walking the tracks, the section men covered many miles each day to ensure safe passage for the trains. There were many during World War One — the freight trains with heavily loaded boxcars and

A helper engine in the middle of a freight train pushes and pulls box cars into the railroad's tunnel on Tunnel Mountain.

A steam engine belches a huge column of white smoke as it chugs up the mountain near Clifton.

A berry picker tries to hitch a ride on a White Pass train near Glacier Station.

flatcars, and the passenger trains with historic parlor cars that carried the tourists. The huge picture windows allowed viewing of the wonderful scenery on the run. There was such a steep grade on the trip north that often three steam engines (one in front, one in the middle, one at the rear) were necessary to pull the heavy loads. Two engines would "deadhead" on the return trip downgrade. One engine would take empty cars back to Skagway for reloading.

Mother took many pictures and felt disappointed that she could not get a full-length train in focus from a distance. They always were going in or out of snow sheds and tunnels or crossing bridges and trestles.

A freight train steams across the steel cantilever bridge. When constructed in 1901, it was the tallest bridge of its kind in the world.

Some rock slides occurred, and often a few rocks would remain on the roadbed as the slide continued on down the mountain to the river.

Occasionally, when we were exploring the ruins of the Klondike Gold Rush trail, we would come to a rock slide. Getting over jagged rocks at a steep angle to get back on the trail was hazardous. Other debris spoke silently of its tragic reason for being there. One slide is very vivid in my mind.

There had been unseasonably heavy rains that August. A rock slide hit a train at Mile 15.6, burying Engine No. 68 and three box cars. The two men in the engine were killed. R.D. "Bert" McKenzie was the engineer. The fireman was his son, Walter McKenzie.

In 1917 early wall models of telephones were in use in Skagway and along the railroad line. Turning the crank for the desired number of rings would place the call on the line of many parties. No one expected nor wanted privacy. All receivers along the line would come down in unison. How else could one get the news? And there was always a possibility that someone was sick or injured and in need of help.

Sharing hardships was an integral part of frontier life. That day the news was bad, and it spread quickly down the mountain. Railroad historian Carl E. Mulvihill says the

ENGINEER AND FIREMAN KILLED WHEN ROCK SLIDE HITS WHITE PASS TRAIN

W. C. McKenzie and Son Bert Killed---No One Else Hurt---Engine and 3 Box Cars Fall Down Embankment Into Valley Below

A rock slide of tremendous violence struck Train No. 1 this morning while it was enroute from Skagway to Whitehorse and between snowshed 15a and the big steel bridge, tearing engine No. 68 and three box cars completely off the track, sending them a half mile down a step embankment to the valley below, and killing Engineer W. C. McKenzie and his son, Fireman Bert McKenzie. The body of the engineer has been recovered. None of the passengers or other employes was injured.

Happened At 11:30 A. M.

The accident happened about 11:30 o'clock this morning, while the train was pushing up the steep grade in mile 15. The train was composed of both freight and passenger cars, the freight train being ahead and the coaches coming last. Two box cars immediately preceding the engine were torn from the track and one box car coming behind the engine and carrying the mail was swept down into the valley.

15 Passengers On Train

About 15 passengers were on the train at the time of the accident, and they have been taken back to the station at Glacier and will be transferred tonight to train No. 2, and proceed on to Whitehorse.

Dr. Gabie, Superintendent V. I. Hahn and many laborers were rushed on a special engine to the scene of the accident this morning and are ready to give any assisance they can. The engine is so far down in the valley that it is impossible to be recovered.

First Fatal Accident

This is the first fatal accident that has occurred on the White Pass since its construction and the accident today was no fault of the company.

The large freight train which was coupled to the passenger train and proceeded it passed safely over the location, and it was just merely chance that the slide struck the engine and freight cars and not the passenger coaches.

In Steep Part of Route

The accident took place in one of the steepest parts of the White Pass Route, and should the coaches have been struck there would have been no chance but for them to have met the fate of the engine.

Mrs. McKenzie, who is now left entirely alone, having lost both husband and son, has the heart felt sympathies of the entire community. Her husband and son were well known throughout the entire Northland, and were loved by all who knew them.

News clip from *Daily Alaskan*, August 28, 1917

victims of the August 28, 1917 accident were buried in Skagway.

On the happy side, we shared many joyful occasions with friends of the grandparents and the children who were invited to Glacier and Clifton for parties.

The 1913 party at Glacier was quite an event. Such a dear picture. Brother, who was almost five, still had his ringlet curls, which he hated and were shorn in time for him to start kindergarten in the fall of that year. How interesting were the different modes of children's dress then. And the expressions on their faces — some are so very serious, and some appear wondering if they should smile, but it seems most decided against that, judging from their sweet, serious reflections picked up by the camera lens.

One wonders where they are now. Could some still be living in Alaska after these 75 years that have passed so quickly? I wish Mother had put the names on the backs of the prints from that party at Glacier, and also on that picture of Brother and his friends taken on the platform at Clifton Station in 1917.

Wise parents and grandparents know that children need other children. They provided us with this contact on several occasions during our visit.

A children's party at Glacier Station on the WP&YR in 1913.

The day the wilderness boys came to visit was a memorable one.

They ranged in ages from five to twelve and each carried his own rifle, geared to his size. They marched up the tracks in military fashion. Grandmother introduced them to us and the soldiers.

"Your sharpshooter boys were Clarence, Chester and Chubby Cartwright," wrote Carl Mulvihill in a letter to me. "Their father was Charlie and years later he was caretaker for the White Pass Athletic Club in Skagway... They lived south of Clifton, but in a small house between Mile 6 (Denver) and Mile 7 (Rocky Point). No one could remember the mother."

On the day of their visit I stood at a distance as they took their firearms from their shoulders and stood them in the corner of the room. I have always been fearful of guns and rifles.

The boys were large for their ages and very strong. Every day they cut firewood and hauled it to the train stop, where it was loaded and taken into Skagway to be exchanged for staple or sold. The echoes of their rifle shots resounded through the ravine as they hunted game. Each was an excellent marksman. Meat from the red squirrels was used

Brother Michael and friends on the platform at Clifton Station in 1917.

for making stew, and the pelts were sold.

The soldiers on guard duty at Clifton were skilled in marksmanship and had their medals. This inevitably led to competition. An improvised target was set up, and much to the military boys' chagrin, they were out-classed by even the youngest brother.

Their special performance following the competition was absolutely against the request and discipline of the grandparents, but the brothers stubbornly insisted. We were very fearful and knew it wasn't right. A can was placed on the head of the youngest, and the oldest shot the can from his brother's head.

One of the boys had seen the jar of yeast bubbling away on the cook range. He asked if there were little devils in the jar. He didn't understand that flour had to have fermentation to turn it into bread. They stayed for supper and enjoyed every bite of that sumptuous meal, regardless of the imaginary devil bubbles in the yeast that helped make the bread.

After supper the soldiers and boys shook hands, and those rugged little pioneers marched down the track with rifles over their erect shoulders and homemade loaves of bread in their knapsacks.

A picnic with the soldiers from Fort Seward on July 29, 1917.

Pitchfork Falls, a favorite snapshot spot for tourists traveling on the White Pass.

Numerous waterfalls tumbled from great heights down the mountains near us. Tourist trains would stop while sightseers feasted their eyes on the cascading grandeur before them.

The Pitchfork Falls at Mile 9 were especially interesting. A sign there said, "WP&Y Route — Pitchfork Falls. Alaska — 460 miles south of the Arctic Circle. Road built 1898-1900. This is one of the many scenic spots en route to Dawson, Fairbanks and points of the lower Yukon River."

There was one place high in the mountains where tourists would get off the train to view the deep ravines between the mountains and see where Skagway was located at the end of Lynn Canal. It was called Inspiration Point (Mile 17), and one could see a distance of fifty miles.

There were lakes at the tops of some of those mountains. The heavy rains and other conditions, probably heavy snow from the previous winter, created too much water on the mountain that fronted the station. One night a flash flood came rushing down toward us. The building we called home remained intact while the waters veered to either side, changing channels as debris piled onto the railroad tracks and road bed. No one could sleep while envisioning the possibility of another rush of cascading waters.

There were many porcupines under the station house. They gnawed at the wood foundation, and the sound was more annoying than usual for those who couldn't sleep that night. But I loved the noise of the waterfalls and didn't mind at all the rather monotonous grind of the little creatures' teeth as they chewed away.

We had grown used to them along with all the other animals and creatures of the wild who shared this beautiful forest home.

The only times we resented the porcupines were when Dog Gyp would come home with his tongue and mouth full of quills. One adult would have to hold him down while another took pliers and pulled the quills out. Poor Gyp would howl and Brother and I would cry. It was quite a disturbing scene. If only Gyp had learned from bitter experience, but he never did.

Porcupines are quite charming little creatures if one stays at a distance. If, when meeting one on the trail, it buries its head down and turns its rear, that means it's time for you to make a hasty retreat. However, they will be loving and faithful pets once their fears are allayed and their confidence and affection keep them from releasing the quills. The quills can be very dangerous and painful once they start working through an area of flesh and into the body. Watching porcupines with field glasses from a distance is quite enjoyable as they wiggle their comical, little bewhiskered faces.

There was one woodsy creature named a marmot which

would sit up on its hind legs and whistle. We wondered what the whistle meant. Was it to call a mate, or a signal to other whistlers? We never knew.

We loved the trains and felt great pride as we watched those sturdy iron horses slowly pulling their loads up the steep grades — smoke spiraling into the sky.

We enthusiastically waited for mail and supplies with anticipation and had to go about a quarter of a mile to the water tank to receive them while the engines took on water. Mail and lighter, unbreakable things could be thrown out to the platform while the northbound train moved slowly up the steep grade fronting the station.

The soldier boys living at the station were mostly young boys who had never been away from their homes in the southern states. They were well-mannered and very homesick and spoke with southern accents. Each two would be there a month and then would be replaced by another two. They never forgot having been received into our family, and many years later Grandmother heard from them via cards and greetings. They thrived on her motherly interest, her homemade breads, biscuits and blueberry pies.

Berry-picking excursions and picnics were happy combinations. Wild raspberries, high and low bush cranberries and blueberries were in abundance. Constant daylight and rich soil and moisture contributed to their size and juiciness.

On berry-picking trips, the pushcar doubled for a picnic table. Cans of berries adorned the table out of reach of

A berry-picking picnic along side the railroad tracks near Skagway.

some cumbersome young bear. Dog Gyp always joined in the expeditions, and we tried to keep him away from the porcupine's habitats.

One day a crewman on his day free from road work and one of the soldier boys piloted us on a daring and dangerous pushcar adventure.

We crossed over what I believe at the time was supposed to be the highest trestle in the world. The picture shows all of us huddled together. There was nothing to hang onto but one another as we crossed it. I cried all the way over and all the way back. My childhood and younger years are filled with examples of fear of heights. Mother knew this but did not want to leave me alone while they took such a chance.

I know the source of this fear. When I was a small child we would go on picnics into the hills surrounding our home town in Idaho. I would be fine while ascending, but the descent was always tortuous. I would cry and sympathetic Daddy would tie his handkerchief around my eyes and lead me down. Bless his memory, but only if he had said, "Now dear, don't mind. You won't fall. Go down the same way you came up — one step at a time." But he didn't and height sensitiveness has been a handicap for me all through life.

To this day, I feel dizzy when I think about that pushcar trip over the trestle. On a recent train trip, when in high places or crossing a high bridge, I had to close my eyes.

5

Exploring the Route of the Gold Seekers

The gold rush "Trail of '98" followed the river closely in many places, and the rotting corduroy of the Brackett Wagon Road still remained in 1917.

The corduroy was caved in at places, but for one year it was a highway for gold seekers. The Brackett road had served for the transit of men and pack horses in 1898. Prior to the building of the road, a crude trail was the only transportation link. Many horses perished. We found toppled grave markers and the bones and carcasses of horses everywhere.

The noble creatures of the "Dead Horse Trail" struggled through jagged rocks and deep snow, carrying loads that were far too heavy and suffered from neglect, mistreatment and not enough to eat. The men had brought it upon themselves — the horses hadn't. Oh, the pity and sadness of it! The horses in our lives in Idaho had always been our faithful friends — well-groomed, fed, loved and cared for.

We had been told the stories of the Klondike Gold Rush and were interested in finding the ruins of old White Pass City at the foot of Dead Horse Gulch, the final ascent to the summit of the White Pass. Located in the valley below the railroad about five miles up the line from Clifton, the old "city" was surrounded by underbrush. We cautiously waded through grass as tall as us to find it.

The old Brackett Wagon Road, with its log corduroy and many bridges still intact in 1917, was a fascinating link to the great gold rush of 1898. Huberta and her family explored many miles of the road, which was built and maintained by George Brackett, a former mayor of Minneapolis, Minnesota. He operated it in 1897-98. The road was purchased by a British investment group as a supply route for building a railroad grade. There was no need for the road after the WP&YR was completed.

Everything that had been left behind at White Pass City was intact enough to investigate. We found deteriorated mattresses, and pans and other utensils hanging on the rusty nails. Racks for drying meat still stood in the tall grasses, and we found the ruins of what must have been a dance floor. Everything that could have been discarded to cut down on pack loads had been left behind and perhaps forgotten. Treacherous White Pass summit was ahead.

This place spoke to us of people from the past, their dreams and their disappointments. Many had perished on the trail, and many had turned back — never reaching Lake Bennett to build their boats and float down the Yukon River to Dawson City and the Klondike gold fields. The hardships suffered by the prospectors must have been excruciating. Few actually made it to the Klondike, and fewer struck it rich.

One day in the summer of 1917, Grandfather found time away from his duties to visit old White Pass City with us. We were investigating the inside of an old cabin which was about ready to topple after nineteen years of weathering the changing seasons. He put his hand into the pocket of a mackinaw that was ready to fall to pieces and took out a poke of gold nuggets.

The picnickers stand in the tall grass among ruins at White Pass City.

Grandfather Rourke stands by a lone grave of a Klondike stampeder at White Pass City.

Grandfather had not taken part in the mad rush for gold. His life had always been railroading, so it is no wonder that he chose the White Pass and Yukon Railroad in Alaska for his last years of employment. He loved the country, and his life there was one of peace, fulfilling his duties, reading and exploring. We always felt fortunate when he returned to Idaho for a visit, especially if we were able to keep him for longer than a week. He could hardly wait until time to return.

On his way to Idaho he would stop at Soap Lake, Washington for bathing to help his rheumatism. The water there always turned his hair red, and we would lovingly tease him about it. In 1925, when he came "out" for the last time to Seattle on account of failing health, I don't think he believed he would ever return to his Alaska. He passed away in Seattle that year, very homesick for his beloved adopted land and the White Pass and Yukon Railroad.

Having exhausted all possibilities of delving into historical and geological attractions near our local base, we took the train to Bennett, British Columbia. The railroad had been completed to the shores of Lake Bennett (Mile 40.6) in July, 1899, ending the need for the Brackett road. The WP&YR became the northern supply route and was completed to Whitehorse a year later. After the gold rush, it became a popular tourist train.

In 1917 ships arrived in Skagway as part of a ten-day excursion trip through the Inside Passage. On arrival in Skagway, tourists would shop and see the sights, then take the awe-inspiring train trip to Bennett. More sightseeing and a scrumptious dinner awaited. A southbound train from Whitehorse picked up some of the tourists for the return trip to Skagway and their ships. Others opted to continue on the northbound train to Carcross and Whitehorse.

The skeleton remains of the Presbyterian Church at Bennett stood on a knoll at the head of the large lake. The church's mute testimony signified that despite their mad pursuit for gold, those rugged men and women had not forgotten to build a place for prayer.

The little boat house that had been used for the construction of boats was still standing intact. More than seven thousand left Bennett when the ice broke in May, 1898 to navigate down the Yukon.

The train continued along the shoreline of Lake Bennett for about thirty miles until we reached Carcross in the Yukon. We visited friends, and as usual it was socially rewarding. We were always received hospitably and served delicious raspberry "shrub," a punch made from concentrated juice. Wild raspberries grew in abundance in many places in that area of Alaska and the Yukon. The delightful English tea cakes served with the punch made a nice combination. How sweet was the tone of the little organ that had been brought from England. I loved to play on it.

We traveled further to Atlin, British Columbia, which was a most interesting trip, though it rained all the time. Mother was not able to get the pictures we would have liked. We spent much time inside the cozy Atlin Inn which cheered our dampened spirits and mood. At Atlin we purchased postcards which showed the beauty of the lake

Grandfather Rourke stands in front of the old Presbyterian Church at Bennett, B.C. Stampeders built the church in 1898, but it was never finished — a victim of the rush for gold. It still stands today, and is being maintained by Parks Canada as part of the Klondike Gold Rush-Chilkoot Trail International Historical Park.

The view of the church overlooking Lake Bennett has not changed much since this photo was taken in 1917. However, the other buildings are long gone. Trees now shelter campsites for modern-day Chilkoot Trail hikers who have completed their journeys.

The tiny "Duchess" steams across a little bridge. The engine ran on a two-mile road that connected boat travelers between the lakes.

and the reflections of the mountains clearly.

I had remembered the boat trips we took to reach Atlin with what Brother and I always called the "Pixie Train" connecting the land between the boats.

The little railroad, according to historian Carl Mulvihill, went by several names — Taku Tram, Taku Central Railway and Atlin Southern — and was operated by the White Pass and Yukon. It was a two-mile line between Taku City on Lake Tagish and Scotia Bay on Lake Atlin. Steamer service from Carcross to Taku was provided by the *Gleaner*, *Australian* and, after 1917, by the *Tutshi*. From Scotia Bay to Atlin, the lake trip was made by the *Scotia* and later by the *Tarahne*.

The Atlin Southern's first engine was the "Duchess," built by Baldwin Locomotive Works in 1878. It was lots of fun riding in the tiny, canvas-covered cars pulled by the "Duchess." We never forgot how, as we went through much greenery, the rain-drenched branches tapped a serenade on the tops of the cars.

The little engine worked the line from 1900 to 1919, when she was retired. The "Duchess" now sits regally on the tracks at Carcross near the remains of the *Tutshi*, which was destroyed by fire in 1990. Would she rather be pulling the little cars along the route? I think so. Old engines never die.

She was replaced by Engine 51 until 1932, and then No. 52 came in to replace the 51, working until 1940. Old 52 was the first engine used on the WP&YR. Built around

The mountains across from Atlin are beautifully reflected in the lake in this postcard from the 1917 trip.

The *Tarahne* took us across Lake Atlin. It still sits on the shore of the lake in historic Atlin, where local people have begun to restore her.

1881, she had worked in Washington state before being taken to Alaska. No. 52 was placed into service out of Skagway in July, 1898. Originally a wood-burning locomotive with a tall, bulging smokestack, the 52 was later converted to a coal-burner by changing the stack. Long ago retired, the trustworthy old iron horse now rests in Skagway across from the rail depot.

6

Summer of Magic

Brother and Dog Gyp

After our return to our base at Clifton, we realized with regret that we soon had to leave to get back to Idaho and the opening of school's fall term. We didn't want to think about leaving and spent as much time as possible in the warmth of the outdoors.

Those adventure-filled months had slipped away all too fast in the land of the midnight sun. Sleep had seemed a waste of time for two lively, curious children. "Why go to bed when it's still light?" was our constant plea. The long hours when darkness never came had been filled with seeking and finding such wonderful places and things.

It was almost time for our return home from the magic of Alaska. Brother had guarded his secret well, but the time had come for him to share it with me.

"Little Sis!" came the subdued voice from across the tracks.

It was a pleasantly warm afternoon and I wanted to finish the book I was reading. I didn't reply.

"Little Sis! Little Sis!"

I roused myself and said, "Yes?"

Dog Gyp was dozing nearby. We could never tell if Gyp was really sleeping. His right eye was blind, and he would lie on his left side, so the totally blank eye would be visible. He lost the eye fighting with a timber wolf while protecting Grandfather.

When I left to go across the tracks to Brother, Gyp hadn't moved. As I approached the rock, little Michael peeked from around the back and said, "Come here!" I followed him around to his secret rendezvous.

"Is Gyp still sleeping?" he whispered. "If he follows you here, he might bark. That would scare my fairies, and big men might find out about my crystal cavern. They would cut it away to get the jewels inside, and my fairies wouldn't like that. They wouldn't have a home anymore, and they might get hurt if they couldn't get away in time."

I was sure I was a bit too old to believe in fairies and a crystal fairy home, but I was delighted with such fantasy and kept real quiet. He beckoned me toward a small opening in the rock wall. It was not more than six inches wide and about three inches high.

"Now wait until the sun shines right straight in the hole — then look real fast!" he instructed me.

The sun's rays moved toward a direct focus. "Now look real quick! Don't stand too close. If you do, the fairies will see you and it will get dark inside. They'll blow their magic candles out."

I did exactly as he said and shall never forget the beauty of what I saw. I beheld a panoramic fairyland of iridescent colors. Hundreds of flickering jewels danced in all directions and at every angle.

I had thought I was too old to believe in fairy folk, but that day I decided there might be fairies. After all, if darkness never came in this magic land, then why couldn't there be fairies and crystal caves too?

Every afternoon that the sun shone before our departure, I went with Brother to a matinee performance in the crystal cavern.

Did the peek hole to the crystal cave expose valuable minerals inside? Were there other veins of minerals there besides the usual crystal reflections we had in our granite rocks back in Idaho?

A fishing trip to "Second Portage" on the WP&YR between the summit and Bennett netted a big catch of grayling. Grandfather waves to us from his favorite fishing spot.

That rock wall had been created when men cut through the solid rock formation to make way for the roadbed of the White Pass and Yukon Railroad. Had we made a strike?

We kept our silence. Fairies and crystal caves mustn't be interfered with, our childhood reasoning told us.

Such was the last adventure of that glorious summer of 1917. It was time to start packing. I was already thinking about the essays I would write for grammar and English classes to let my classmates know about Alaska. Most everyone in our town had thought we would be going to a land of ice and snow and riding every place on dog sleds. How surprised they would be to learn how different it had been. We hadn't seen one igloo like those pictured in our geography books, and the only dog sleds we saw were from the pictures in Grandfather's album. If we had visited in winter, it would have been different, but getting out of the heat of a southeastern Idaho summer into the mild atmosphere of a southeastern Alaska summer had been heavenly.

We had promised to be brave children and not cry when the time came to leave. As the boat pulled away from its mooring at the Skagway dock, we bit our lips and tried to smile while waving our handkerchiefs and throwing kisses. We left our beloved grandparents standing there with dear Gyp beside them.

Much to our dismay, we found we were on a boat which would stop at fish canneries and load salmon on the way back to Seattle. A trip that ordinarily took four days turned into an eight-day cruise. The change in plans turned into an educational experience. There was much time to spend on shore, and we explored the canneries and Indian villages.

When we finally arrived in Seattle, Daddy was waiting patiently for us. We were already late for the opening day of school.

EPILOGUE

As I relive these glorious memories of 1917, and now add the memories of my recent trip back to Alaska after 71 years, my heart overflows with love for our dear grandparents who made the summer of 1917 possible; thankfulness for wonderful Mother who took the pictures and turned each experience into one of learning; and gratitude for a dear Dad who unselfishly loaned us to Alaska for those magic months while he labored in railroading in the heat of an Idaho summer.

We had planned to return together, hadn't we Brother, but you were taken away in 1981. I took the trip alone in 1988, but your presence seemed so near. Thank you dear one for all the happy hours we spent together reminiscing the happenings of that wonderful summer.

Now I feel that our dedication to the memory of the dear ones who provided us such happiness and learning is complete in the pages of this book. I can get on to writing my tribute to you and your thirty-five years as Michael O'Rourke of the world famous puppeteers of Walton and O'Rourke.

They were years of adventures and unusual happenings, weren't they? One time you and your partner, Paul E. Walton, did a command performance at Christmas for Princess Grace and her children at the Royal Palace of

Monaco. You also entertained for royalty in England. Your regimen of credits from all over the world are too numerous to enumerate here, but you always remained the same unassuming, kind, sensitive and thoughtful one your Sis knew so well.

You wore your crown humbly in life and made your exit smiling into death. You requested that your remains be put out to sea, the sea you loved with a passion. How you loved the Inside Passage to Skagway in 1917. We both did.

Huberta Swensen and Michael O'Rourke Professional Name

Huberta Nanney Swensen
Charles Carlyle Nanney

To order more copies of this book, please write:

Lynn Canal Publishing
P.O. Box 1898
Skagway, Alaska 99840-0498